A Pictorial Guide To

AMERICAN SPINNING WHEELS

By

David A. Pennington
And
Michael B. Taylor

Cover Design And Photographs
By
James P. Munsie

The Shaker Press
Sabbathday Lake, Maine
1975

Copyright © 1975 by David A. Pennington
Library of Congress Catalogue Card Number 75-15298
ISBN 0-915836-01-7
Printed and Bound in the United States of America
Produced at Pen-Mor Printers, Inc., Lewiston, Maine

Contents

Preface

Our introduction to spinning wheels occurred when Dave Pennington's wife, Beth, learned to spin wool for her weaving. Soon thereafter the Pennington's home began to groan under the influx of wheels and parts of wheels. Dave's initial interest was in how the different types worked. Having satisfied his mechanical curiosity, he began to wonder how old the wheels were and where they came from. The initials and names he found marked on some of his wheels provided the first clues along with certain recurrent styles which he thought must be regional or national. At that point Mike and Cindy Taylor became quite interested in the project. Since that fateful meeting in 1969, the four of us have owned more than 200 spinning wheels and have traveled all over the country visiting museums and other collectors examining wheels and gathering information. It soon became apparent that while the spinning wheel may be the traditional symbol for antique dealers, very little is known about the history of the spinning wheel in the United States.

Several museum curators and many antique dealers have encouraged us to make available the information we have. Recognizing the fragmentary nature of the information, we have decided to rely heavily on photographs to convey the diversity of styles which characterize the American spinning wheel. At this point we know something about regional and national differences, some about dating wheels, and a lot about the diversity of wheels. Some of our most typical American styles are modifications of European styles. Others are true examples of American ingenuity. We have included pictures of a number of European wheels both to show the roots of the American spinning wheel and to show what is now being imported which can be confusing to antique dealers and spinning wheel buyers.

Several persons and organizations have been particularly generous with their time and assistance. We would like to thank the people at the Merrimack Valley Textile Museum for all their many kindnesses which are

1

far beyond one's fondest hopes. The kindness and help of the Shaker community at Sabbathday Lake have been most appreciated. David Serette has been particularly generous with his time and expertise in the trials of publication. We are grateful for the encouragement of Ted Johnson and Sister Mildred Barker of that community. Above all, however, we must thank Marion Channing, whose books opened up the marvelous world of spinning to us. She has supplied us with information and fine food on more occasions than we can ever repay.

The superb photography which tells far more than our ponderous prose is the artistry of Jim Munsie. Jim has been bitten badly by the spinning wheel bug, which may account for the obvious love of subject his pictures show. We are all in his debt.

We hope that this book will help antique dealers, spinning wheel collectors, museum curators, and spinners to recognize what they have. If in the process we shed some light on the development of the spinning wheel in the United States, then so much the better. We hope you enjoy this book as much as we have enjoyed collecting the material for it.

Please feel free to contact us for information about wheels you have. If you will send several pictures of the wheel and rubbings of any marks on it we will attempt to identify the wheel as to origin and date. Please address all inquires to:

Mr. David A. Pennington
1993 W. Liberty
Ann Arbor, Michigan 48103

Introduction

In talking with people about spinning wheels, we have found that there are two major stumbling blocks to making ourselves understood; terminology and the mechanics of spinning wheels. In order to facilitate the reader's understanding of how a spinning wheel works and what the various parts are called, we have included labelled pictures of the two basic types of wheels, flax and wool, as well as a verbal description of the parts of a spinning wheel and how they function. The reader can refer to these pictures when helpful. We have included a chapter with pictures and descriptions of other textile tools which might be confused with spinning wheels or which might be of interest to a collector of spinning equipment. In this way we hope to remedy existing misinformation about spinning wheels and make the rest of our book more helpful.

Not surprisingly, all the spinning wheels we will be discussing have at least one wheel. The *wheel* supplies the power to the spinning mechanism via a *driving cord*. The wheel is supported by the *wheel supports*. The wheel supports originate in the *table*. The table in turn rests on three or more *legs*. Some unusual spinning wheels do not have tables as such, but we will consider these wheels in detail later. The last thing common to both flax and wool wheels is a *tension device* for the driving cord. The tension device tightens the driving cord by moving the spinning mechanism away from the wheel.

The spinning mechanisms on the wool wheel and the flax wheel are fundamentally different as are the way they are supported; so it will probably be helpful to refer to Fig. 1 at this point. The spinning mechanism on a wool wheel is a metal spike or *spindle*. The wool is spun off the tip of the revolving spindle. The spindle is usually held onto the *head* by braided *corn husks*. The head is supported on the *spindle post* which originates in the table as does the wheel support. There are several different types of spindle heads and tension devices among wool wheels, and we cover these differences in our chapter on wool wheels.

3

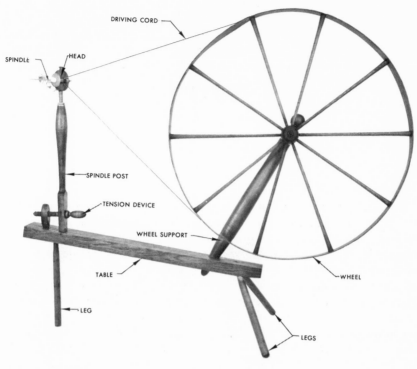

DRIVING CORD

SPINDLE   HEAD

SPINDLE POST

TENSION DEVICE

WHEEL SUPPORT

TABLE

LEG

WHEEL

LEGS

FIGURE 1
   Wool Wheel
Munsie Collection

The spinning mechanism on the flax wheel is the *bobbin and flyer.* This apparatus not only spins the flax by means of the flyer, but also winds the spun flax on the bobbin at the same time. This combination of functions in the flax wheel is a great advantage over the wool wheel. The spinner using the wool wheel must stop spinning and wind the spun wool on the spindle in a momentary but separate operation. For this reason spinning on a wool wheel is called discontinuous, and spinning on a flax wheel is called continuous. The bobbin and flyer are supported between two posts called *maidens* by *leathers* made of leather. The maidens sit in the *mother-of-all* which is a part of the tension device. The flax wheel also features a *foot treadle* which allows the spinner to sit while operating the wheel unlike the wool wheel. The foot treadle is connected to the *axle crank* by a *footman.* In this manner foot power is translated into wheel revolutions. Normally, flax wheels have a *distaff* set in the table which holds the supply of unspun flax.

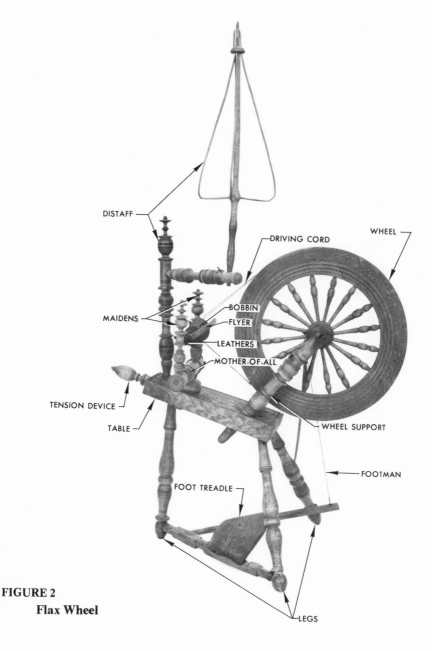

DISTAFF

DRIVING CORD

WHEEL

MAIDENS

BOBBIN

FLYER

LEATHERS

MOTHER-OF-ALL

TENSION DEVICE

TABLE

WHEEL SUPPORT

FOOTMAN

FOOT TREADLE

LEGS

FIGURE 2
Flax Wheel

Pennington Collection

5

The preceding discussion of wheel parts and their functions should enable the reader to recognize and name these main parts of the spinning wheel. Obviously this description will not enable one to spin wool or flax, but there are several good books on that subject which are listed in our bibliography.

In the ensuing chapters we will illustrate and describe the different types and styles of spinning wheels. It is most fascinating to watch how various people tried to solve the same problems posed by the spinning of wool or flax into yarn or thread. We will start with European wheels and move through the variety of wheels found in this country culminating in a sampling of the hosts of patent wheels made at the end of the 19th century when handspinning was in its final stages in this country. Finally, we show some examples of textile tools used in conjunction with spinning wheels.

Chapter One

European Wheels

If you were to walk into an antique store and see the small flax wheel pictured in Fig. 3, you might be told any of the following: "it just came over on a boat from Germany"; "it is an old American wheel"; "it is a reproduction". Strangely enough on this particular wheel any of these statements could be true. We have seen wheels virtually identical to this one which fall into all three categories. Dave has repaired nearly fifteen such wheels brought back from Germany by collectors. Others have been purchased from individuals who can remember their grandmothers using these wheels at the turn of this century. One of these was stamped "Monroe, Michigan" and was probably produced in that city. A very similar wheel is pictured in an advertisement for spinning wheels in a German-speaking newspaper published in Milwaukee, Wisconsin in 1894. We have recently seen a reproduction of this wheel in the Midwest. All of this points out the difficulty in ascertaining the precise origin of any particular spinning wheel of this style. It also indicates that some of the people who made wheels in the United States produced wheels like the ones found in the country from which they or their families had emigrated. (A word of warning to spinners at this point is important. Many of the reproductions of this type have bobbins and flyers which are too crude to be functional.) The spinning wheel in Fig. 3 was found in Dundee, Michigan. It was one of eight found in that city, all nearly identical. This fact leads us to believe that these wheels were produced in this country by people of German ancestry.

The wheel pictured in Fig. 4 is reminiscent of wheels coming from Eastern European countries. It too could have been made in this country by or for an immigrant, but the style is very definitely Eastern European. The similarity between it and the German style wheel in Fig. 3 is quite noticeable. The main difference is in the treadles. The German wheel uses a leather hinge while the wheel in Fig. 4 uses the more common rotating wooden treadle bar.

7

FIGURE 3

This German style flax wheel is pictured without a distaff. This particular wheel has a hole in the table to accommodate a distaff assembly. Some wheels of this style do not. In Europe they often used a free standing distaff for their flax wheels, which would account for the missing hole in the table in some cases. When this style was adapted to wool spinning in the late 19th century, there was no need for a distaff assembly. Large hooks and a large orifice are the best indications that a wheel was of this later type. The chapter on Canadian wheels gives more information about such transitional types. Most wheels of this German style were for spinning flax. Note that the treadle uses a leather hinge which is typical of many wheels coming from countries with a Germanic heritage.

(Pennington Collection)

8

FIGURE 4

This European wheel with a steep incline to the table strongly suggests a Polish wheel shown in the Horner collection of European wheels. It has no hole for a distaff assembly. The treadle uses the more typical rotating treadle bar arrangement. The turnings on the legs are more European than American in style. The hook shown dangling from a string is original and typical of the type used for feeding the linen or woolen thread through the orifice. (Pennington Collection)

Obviously, one would not want to stake one's life on the nationality of a wheel on such a slight difference; and yet, often the clues to origin are as slight as this treadle difference.

In Figs. 5 and 6 we see two wheels found in this country which are distinguishable by their very thick wheel rims. This wide rim is very characteristic of Dutch spinning wheels. These wheels are better spinners than the first two wheels shown in this chapter due to the additional momentum provided by the heavier wheels, making them easier to treadle. Other wheels we will see later also have sought to increase wheel momentum through such means

9

as heavy rims of various metals, larger diameter wheels, and heavy turnings on the spokes near the wheel rims.

The spinning wheel pictured in Fig. 7 has more names than a flim-flam man. It is variously called a parlor wheel, cottage wheel, traveling wheel, castle wheel, and probably others we have not yet heard. For no particular reason other than habit we will call this style a castle wheel. This type is found all over Europe. John Horner, whose collection of European wheels is well known in this country, refers to this style as the German style, but he shows them coming from Great Britain and Russia and most of the countries in between. The distinguishing feature of this style is the driving wheel set under the bobbin and flyer. The one pictured is somewhat atypical in that it has an exceptionally large driving wheel. Many of these spinning wheels are being imported. It was not a popular style in this country because of the small driving wheel which made the spinner treadle rapidly. It is among wheels of this type that one is more likely to find metal wheel rims to increase momentum.

Our favorite spinning wheel is the Irish Castle wheel pictured in Fig. 8. This type of wheel has no table, which makes it unusual among spinning wheels. It is shown in Horner's collection, and he found many of them in the Ulster area of Ireland, hence its name. Interestingly enough a man named Danner was making these in Manheim, Pennsylvania in the 1830's. The particular one pictured in Fig. 8 is attributed to him, and others with his label on them are known to us. Since it is reasonable to assume that he was not Irish and lived in Pennsylvania Dutch territory, we wonder how he came to make this style of spinning wheel. It is one of our favorite unanswered questions about American spinning wheels. The Irish Castle wheel is definitely one of the more unusual wheels and is particularly attractive. It is one of the few spinning wheels which has the driving wheel located above the bobbin and flyer.

The little spinning wheel pictured in Fig. 9 is commonly found in the Normandy area of France. Variations of this style with its triangular base are found throughout France, and a similar style with a rectangular base is found in Germany, Italy, and Switzerland. Horner called this style Tyrolean. It suffers from the same mechanical shortcoming we mentioned with regard to small Castle wheels, namely a small driving wheel. We have seen one such Tyrolean wheel with a pewter insert in the rim of the wheel to improve this drawback. To date we have not seen a wheel of this style which we have any reason to believe might have been made in the United States.

The wheel pictured in Fig. 10 is one now seen in quantity on the import market. It appears to be Swiss in origin although this style might appear in any Alpine country. This style was made in Switzerland into this century. It normally employs a bobbin and flyer mechanism of a slightly different type than is seen on wheels made in this country. Only the bobbin is powered by

FIGURE 5

This classic Dutch flax wheel with a very thick wheel rim has the ball type turnings often seen in wheels of this type. The small finial shown in the middle of the table is the handle for a swinging lid covering a small dug out compartment in the table. This compartment is often seen in this style of wheel, but its use is still not known to the authors although many interesting suggestions have been made. The last part of the distaff is not original. (Pennington Collection)

11

FIGURE 6

This Dutch type wheel has the decorative half spokes often seen on European wheels. These half spokes are sometimes made of bone or ivory, and we have yet to see them on a wheel of American design. The bobbin rack on the distaff assembly is useful for plying and could be replaced with a distaff when flax was being spun rather than plied. The turnings are not as typical of Dutch wheels as the ball turnings in Figure 5, but the very thick rim places it squarely in the Dutch tradition.

(Pennington Collection)

12

FIGURE 7

This "castle" or parlor wheel is a style seen throughout Europe. The wheel on this particular model is larger than most. Often the wheel is only 8" - 12" in diameter on this style. It is this style of wheel which often has decorative half spokes of ivory or bone. The smaller wheel has little momentum and occasionally they are made with metal rims for better spinning. As a group these wheels are probably the worst for spinning. The distaff is missing on the one shown here.   (Pennington Collection)

FIGURE 8

This Irish castle wheel was made in Mannheim, Penna. by Daniel Danner in the 1830's. Several others by this maker are known. Horner found some near Ulster Ireland, so we assume that the style originated there. In our opinion these are the most beautiful of all spinning wheels. The distaff shown is not original. The tripod base is very stable. Occasionally, a leather hinged treadle rather than a pivoting treadle bar is found on these wheels. The tripod base with the wheel above the bobbin and flyer are the distinguishing features of this style of wheel. (Pennington Collection)

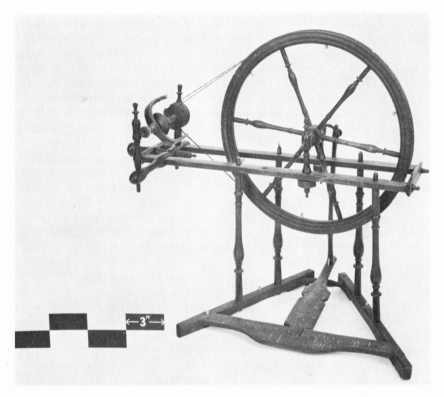

FIGURE 9

This small wheel is found throughout Europe. The one shown has a triangular base which is characteristic of the Normandy area of France. The style has a rectangular base in the Germanic areas of Europe. Note how small this wheel is. It is not a very good spinner. There is no distaff hole. The hole found in the front horizontal bar usually has a metal arm with a water cup for flax spinning. Apparently, this wheel used a free standing distaff. Ivory buttons and pins are often found on these wheels.

(Pennington Collection)

15

FIGURE 10

This Swiss style wheel has no distaff hole. Some were made as late as 1914, and most appear to have been used for wool spinning. It has a lead bobbin and flyer as described in the text. This means there is a pulley on the bobbin but none on the flyer. This style does not appear to have been copied in the United States, but it is being imported in quantity now. (Pennington Collection)

16

the driving cord. Normally on spinning wheels made in America a single driving cord goes around both the bobbin and flyer.

The serious student of spinning wheels would be wise to refer to the small book, *Spinning Wheels: The John Horner Collection,* published by the Ulster Museum. The wheels illustrated there are all European, and there is a description of the several different types of bobbin and flyer mechanisms.[1] We have not included pictures of all the European styles found in the Horner collection. We have shown the ones which have had an impact on the American scene or which are presently being imported. All of the wheels shown in this chapter are flax wheels. European wool wheels are very scarce in this country. To our knowledge we have only seen one. They are very similar in construction to their American counterparts. The reason they were not brought over by immigrants was most likely their size. They were also relatively easy to make, so immigrants made or bought them on their arrival here.

There are a few generalities that we would like to make about European wheels after seeing hundreds. With the exceptions of the Low Dutch wheel and its Irish successor which were the forerunners of our American Saxony flax wheel, European wheels were more ornate in turnings and more delicate in appearance and construction than their American counterparts. As we have noted the driving wheels were generally smaller in diameter and rim depth. The overall size of the spinning wheels is also smaller. Occasionally, European wheels are found made out of fine woods with ivory embellishments, brass wheels, or other non-essential refinements. There are two explanations given for these ornate spinning wheels. The first is they were for the doweries of well-to-do young ladies. The second is that they were a part of a Victorian craze which affected wealthy women who craved to spin. Both explanations probably have some merit to them.

---

1 G.B. Thompson, ed. Spinning Wheels: (The John Horner Collection) (Belfast, 1966), p. 13 and 14. The text contains technical errors in the decription of the function of various flyer and bobbin mechanisms.

FIGURE 11

This very typical New England Flax wheel is very austere. It was found in Harvard, Mass. about one mile from the Shaker settlement there. The distaff shown is not original, but is a type often seen with Shaker wheels. There is no identifying mark on this wheel, so we have not placed it among our Shaker wheels. It may well be Shaker. The legs and wheel supports are more elaborately turned than one would expect from a Shaker wheel.   (Pennington Collection)

18

Chapter Two

Saxony Wheels

The American Saxony flax wheel is the end product of some 250 years of development in Europe. A popular legend attributes the invention of the Saxony style of flax wheel to Master Johann Jurgen of Germany in 1530. It is now clear that the bobbin and flyer mechanism which was supposed to have been his major contribution was on hand as early as 1488. Perhaps as Lynn White hints, Jurgen's true contribution was the treadle and crank combination which freed the hands of the spinner for the first time.[2] This combination of bobbin and flyer, foot treadle and crank reached one of its highest forms in the Dutch wheel which Thomas Wentworth introduced into Ireland in the 1630's. Its superior design and popularity with spinners in Ireland was such that when Louis Crommelin tried to introduce his favorite wheel from his native France in the 1680's, he was totally unsuccessful. This Dutch style with a narrower wheel rim than those pictured in Figs. 5 and 6 appears to have been popular throughout the British Isles. This style of wheel was brought by early colonists to the Northeastern colonies. Fig. 11 is typical of those we now find in the Northeastern United States and is virtually identical to the one shown in Horner's collection as a Dutch or Low Irish wheel. Its popularity in this country persisted until handspinning died out late in the last century and is probably attributable to both its fine spinning qualities and the relative ease with which it could be produced. This Dutch style is now known as the Saxony wheel, purportedly after the area in Germany from which Johann Jurgen came.

The austere looking Saxonys in Figs. 11 and 12, so typical of the Northeastern United States, had its lines somewhat softened as it was copied in the Southern and Midwestern states. Examples of this trend are seen in Figs. 13

2 Lynn White, Jr., Medieval Technology and Social Change. (New York: Oxford University Press, 1962), p. 119.

FIGURE 12

This very plain wheel has "W. Kelia" stamped in the end grain of the table. The wheel is made of quarter-sawn oak as is the table. Most of the New England wheels are made this way. The turned pieces are often maple or birch. The treadles were mostly quarter-sawn oak. The branch type distaff is very common. This is one of the few wheels we have found which is truly complete.   (Pennington Collection)

FIGURE 13

This flax wheel was found in Ohio and shows the similarity between Eastern and Midwestern flax wheels when compared with Figures 11 and 12. The most distinctive difference appears to be in the turnings on the spokes. It is difficult to make a positive identification of a single wheel without comparing it with several other wheels whose provenance is well authenticated. (Pennington Collection)

FIGURE 14

This flax wheel from Ohio has a spoke turning most commonly seen in the Midwest. This wheel is distinctive because of the unusual treadle arrangement which is the reverse of the more common variety. This treadle arrangement throws the wheel back closer to the bobbin and flyer. Two other such wheels from Ohio are known. We know of none with this treadle arrangement which come from the East.

(Pennington Collection)

FIGURE 15

This flax wheel was found in the Midwest and is very elaborately turned. We would hazard a guess that this wheel might have been made in the Philadelphia area, but it may have been made in any sophisticated urban area during the first half of the 19th century. The turnings on the spokes are often found in the East.

(Pennington Collection)

and 14 with its peak reached in Fig. 15. The spinning wheels pictured in Figs. 13 and 14 were purchased in Ohio and are representative of the Saxonies found in the Midwest. They are not exceptional in the craftsmanship exemplified in them. The wheel pictured in Fig. 15 on the other hand shows a high degree of sophistication in design and execution. It was most likely made by a professional wheelmaker for someone who was relatively wealthy. Thus, it is unlikely that such a wheel was made in any frontier area. Many finely made wheels and some not so finely made wheels (even disasters) were wisely or unwisely stamped with the maker's name or initials. Fig. 16. A list of those marks we have observed to date is presented in Appendix A. The number of American Saxonies with minor variations is overwhelming, but we hope that the five we have shown you give you a clear idea of the characteristic look of this style.

American Saxonies are usually called flax wheels as are most spinning wheels with bobbin and flyer mechanisms. It seems likely to us, however, that late in the 19th century some American Saxonies with minor modifications (larger flyer hooks and orifice, and perhaps a different pulley ratio) in the spinning mechanisms were used to spin wool. In our chapter on Canadian spinning wheels you can see the end result of this modification of the Saxony style for the spinning of wool rather than flax. We further prefer to call this style "flax wheels" so as not to confuse the issue.

It is worth noting some of the construction features of spinning wheels found in this country. They do not differ markedly from construction features found in other furniture pieces of the same period. They do have some unique features, such as split or quarter-sawn oak tables to prevent warpage. Since these tables were often left in this unfinished condition, trapezoids, rather than rectangles, are seen when viewing the ends of the tables. A rectangular table end indicates either a more careful craftsman or a more affluent setting and a later date. Virtually all wheels were made for disassembly for ease in moving to their ultimate destination. Thus, we seldom find wedges or pegs which were not meant to be easily removed. For those of us who collect spinning wheels, this happy occurrence has allowed us to transport even the largest wool wheels in very small cars. For easy transportation, the legs and wheels supports were tapered for insertion or removal from tapered holes in the table. Many people have learned about this "jam fit" the hard way by picking up a spinning wheel and having the legs fall out. In stores with "you break it, you pay for it" signs, such an occurrence can be rather rattling. Most commonly, the driving wheel and the table are made out of oak. The other parts, especially turned ones, are usually made of hard woods like maple or birch, but many kinds of woods have been used in the production of spinning wheels.

Some of the great quandaries faced by spinning wheel enthusiasts concern

24

FIGURE 16

"B. Sanford" was a prolific wheel maker in Conn. who made several different styles of wheels. Many makers used a stamp or brand on the tables of their wheels to identify the maker's work. (Pennington Collection)

the production of wheels. Are they the product of individual craftsmen for home consumption or for sale to the public? To what extent were spinning wheels made in small or large factories? Were spare bobbins and flyers made for sale in the local general store as wool wheel heads appear to have been? Since the tools required to make a Saxony style wheel are rather specialized, it seems unlikely that when "Mom" wanted a flax wheel, dear old "Dad" went out to the barn and whipped one up. We know of a well-documented case of a spinning wheel maker named Jeremiah Pike, living in Framingham, Mass. in the 1680's, who employed five or six other men in his operation. His family carried on his business for four generations, nearly 100 years in all. The Shakers, a celibate religious group located in the Northeast and Midwest, made thousands of wool and flax wheels for sale to the public. From the individual names we find stamped on wheels, we assume that there were many small spinning wheel operations with perhaps the craftsman and several apprentices the total work force. Some makers of spinning wheels made several styles of flax and wool wheels. "B. Sanford", for example, appears on three very different styles of wheel, and E.B. Sandford was a patentor of a spinning wheel in 1816. Given the spelling errors in early patent lists, it is quite possible that these two persons are one and the same. At the turn of this century factories producing turned wood products, like brooms, also turned out small quantities of spinning wheels as a side line. Thus, we surmise that both individual craftsmen and factories made spinning wheels, but it is highly unlikely that a person made a spinning wheel of the saxony style solely for his own home. We know also that some companies made nothing but wool wheel heads, but the lack of interchangeability between bobbins and flyers of different wheels leads us to believe that spare bobbin and flyer units were made rarely if at all. However, extra bobbins often accompanied new spinning wheels. They allowed a spinner to fill several bobbins before beginning plying, which required three bobbins or more in most cases.

Every spinning wheel is as individual as the maker's fingerprints.

Naturally, this makes it very difficult to untangle the history of the spinning wheel. Much of that history is irrevocably lost in the fireplaces of past generations. Hopefully, ours and future generations will be more respectful of textile tools and other functional pieces which aren't classified as furniture. It will certainly make the task of the historian of technology easier.

Chapter Three
Unusual Wheels

The next three chapters are devoted to unusual varieties of flax wheels. All these wheels have, at least, one bobbin and flyer unit. They represent some of the early attempts by Americans to make a better spinning wheel. In most cases, however, no one beat a path to their door. Some of those pictured may be unique in style, but most of them represent a style which was at least locally popular.

The wheel pictured in Fig. 17 came from upstate New York, and a similar one is in the Farmer's Museum in Cooperstown, New York. The maker emigrated from New York to Michigan in 1850 and brought the wheel with him. It is missing the distaff assembly. Dave reports that it is a good spinner, and an awkward, but adequate design. The orifice and hooks on the flyer are too small for wool, but very good for flax. It is a most unusual style of wheel in any case.

The "E.S. Williams" wheel is shown in Fig. 18. It has his named stamped on the top of the table. There are, at least two other wheels of the same style with his name on them, which are known to us. A wheel stamped with "J. Farnham" of Owego, New York is very similar in style to the Williams wheel. It is our one good clue as to where this style may have been popular initially.

In Fig. 19 we see an upright flax wheel with a somewhat unusual tension device. The circular post entering the table is threaded into the small block of wood which carries the maidens. When this post is turned, the block moves up or down adjusting the tension on the driving cord. A wheel of very similar design, but with two bobbin and flyer units is seen in Fig. 27. This wheel as those in Figs. 20 and 21 probably represent attempts by their makers to reduce the amount of floor space required to house the wheel.

The wheel in Fig. 20 came out of Pennsylvania Dutch territory; and while the paint is relatively new (perhaps as late as 1900), the wheel is obviously much older. The wheel axle bearings are of brass. Usually, such axle

FIGURE 17

This flax wheel was found in Michigan in a family which had its roots in upstate New York. It is reminiscent of another wheel seen in New York State and has a marked similarity to the wheel shown in Figure 18. The tension device is unusual, and it has an internal crank on the wheel. It is missing its distaff which would be similar to the one shown in Figure 18.   (Pennington Collection)

FIGURE 18

This wheel with "E.S. Williams" stamped on the top of the table is one of three we have seen. It is similar to a wheel made by J. Farnham of Owego, New York. The tension device is the threaded horizontal rod which pushes the supports below the mother-of-all. The top piece of the distaff is not original.   (Pennington Collection)

FIGURE 19

This upright flax wheel has a single bobbin and flyer although most of this style have two as in Figure 27. The turnings on the spoke have a Midwestern flavor, and the wheel was found in Michigan. However, we are sure that wheels of this style were made in the East. Some of these wheels had metal flyers, a feature normally associated with European wheels. We have no indication that wheels of this sort with a four-legged base were made in Europe although they do remind one of the Irish castle wheel with the driving wheel directly above the bobbin and flyer assembly. The threaded rod tension device is distinctly American. (Pennington Collection)

FIGURE 20

This upright wheel came out of Pennsylvania Dutch territory and is painted black and gold. The paint is old but not original and several wheels of this style, unpainted, have been seen in Pennsylvania Dutch areas. It appears to be a style of wheel made only in such areas, and no European counterpart is known. The back maiden has no finial and was constructed that way. (Pennington Collection)

31

FIGURE 21

This American version of the Irish castle wheel shown in Figure 8 was found in Harvard, Mass. It has a much larger wheel than its European counterpart. It is very stable and sturdy. No other examples of this wheel are known.

(Pennington Collection)

FIGURE 22

This painted flax wheel is from Pennsylvania and has some stenciled designs, as well as the name "W.H. Logan" painted on it. The name could be either the makers or the person for whom it was intended. The top part of the distaff is probably not original. A powered quilling attachment may well have been included with this wheel but only hints of its point of attachment and a few pieces not shown remain.

(Pennington Collection)

bearings, if present at all, are made from hard woods, bone, or horn. Other wheels of this style have been reported in Pennsylvania Dutch areas, but they were unpainted.

The variation of the Irish Castle wheel (Fig. 8) seen in Fig. 21 is an American attempt to adapt this style for use in this country. The driving wheel is considerably larger than those found on the typical Irish Castle wheel. This larger wheel corrects the one major drawback of the Irish Castle wheel which was its lack of momentum in the driving wheel. It is somewhat surprising that more of this style of wheel have not yet surfaced. It takes up a minimum amount of floor space, and it is a fine spinner. Its austere look is in keeping with its area of discovery in Harvard, Massachusetts.

The "W.H. Logan" wheel also came out of Pennsylvania and is shown in Fig. 22. The name is painted on. It has stenciling and is painted brown and gold. In styling it is somewhat similar to the wheels in Figs. 24-26. However, its tension device moves the entire top table to which the maidens are fastened. Normally, in wheels of this style only the maidens are moved by the tension device. It is not surprising that only one such tension device is known.

The wheels in this chapter are all unusual in design in a variety of ways. They share two characteristics that caused us to group them together. First, they have only one bobbin and flyer unit unlike those in Chapter Four. Second, they have no accelerating wheels, unlike those wheels pictured in Chapter Five. All of these wheels (Figs. 17-22) were designed to spin flax, but most of the distaffs have been lost although locations for their placement remain.

Chapter Four

Double Flyer Flax Wheels

The spinning wheels pictured in this chapter are known by many names as a result of their double bobbin and flyer units. These wheels are called gossip wheels, two-handed wheels, lover's wheels, mother and daughter wheels, double flyer, and double spindle wheels. The last name is technically incorrect since there are no spindles on these wheels; yet, it is probably the most common.

The idea behind the double flyer wheel is a very old one. It was an attempt to double the production of the spinner. In a pamphlet written by John Firmin in 1681 entitled "Some Proposals for the Imployment of the Poor", the author suggested that these wheels should be used. Firmin indicated that small children should be taught to spin on wheels with single bobbin and flyer units until they were proficient with both hands, and then they could be taught the use of the more efficient two-handed model. A drawing of a double flyer wheel similar to those in Figs. 24-26 is included in Firmin's pamphlet, which was published in London, England. Firmin also suggested that such wheels could be used to spin wool as well as flax, which is the first indication we have of the use of a bobbin and flyer for wool spinning. We know from an illustration in Horner's collection that double flyer wheels were in use on the European continent.

The wheel shown in Fig. 23 is one of four virtually-identical wheels we have seen. One of them was definitely imported from Denmark. The leather hinges on the treadle are suggestive of a German origin, and it is certainly European. We show it here to point out that this improvement was known in Europe but took a slightly different style there.

The wheels in Fig. 24-26 are the most common style of American double flyer wheel. The wheel shown in Fig. 24 was found in Pennsylvania. The ones in Figs. 25-26 were found in New Hampshire and have a slightly different wheel support. This difference does not appear to be regionally specific

FIGURE 23

This European two-handed flax wheel with two bobbins and flyers was intended to be used by one person to increase thread production. It was possible, of course, for two people to use this wheel simultaneously, but this was not the reason for the development of this style of wheel. Two separate driving bands were used on this particular wheel which was not the case with its American counterparts shown in the following figures. The branch distaff is not original. (Pennington Collection)

FIGURE 24

This American two-handed flax wheel is typical of many of this style seen by the authors. It is the most common variant from the saxony flax wheel illustrated in the preceding chapter. The vertical wheel support seems to be more typical of wheels found from New York State west, but examples from New England are known. The turnings on the spoke are Eastern in style. (Pennington Collection)

37

FIGURE 25

This American two-handed flax wheel has a horizontal wheel support. It is complete, and the spike distaff appears typical to this type of wheel. Many wheels of this style are known. "B. Sanford" and "I. Sanford" or "J. Sanford" are either burned or stamped into many wheels of this style. Other makers also put their marks, either initials or names, on this style. Unmarked two-handed wheels are the exception rather than the rule.   (Pennington Collection)

FIGURE 26

This double flyer flax wheel shows the more characteristic turnings found on wheels of this sort. This wheel is unmarked, but it is very similar to the Sanford wheels. Figure 25 was also unmarked, but we have shown these two rather than marked ones because of their completeness and fine condition. (Pennington Collection)

39

FIGURE 27

This double flyer wheel from Conn. is not terribly uncommon. The spoke turnings are Midwestern in flavor, but the finials on the maidens are more Eastern. It is well turned with scorched-in lines for decorations. This type of decoration is common as are chip carvings on tables. (Pennington Collection)

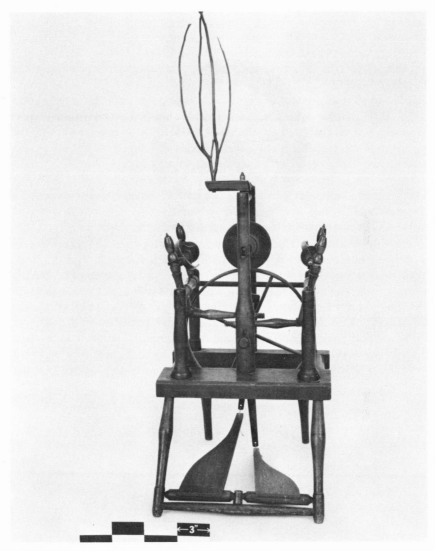

FIGURE 28

This "two-handed wheel" is identical to several wheels stamped "A. Webster" with single bobbin and flyers. Webster made wheels in New York in the early 19th century. This wheel was found in Arizona and has a mesquite distaff indicating that it was used out there. This wheel is the first we have shown with a double treadle arrangement which simplifies treadling enormously. The wheel rim of the larger wheel is metal. The accelerating wheel in the middle is very reminiscent of a Minor's head on a wool wheel.　　　　　　　　　　　　　　　　　　　　　(Pennington Collection)

41

although the horizontal wheel support is more prevalent in the Northeast. Wheels of this style are fairly plentiful indicating that some of our forebearers were very talented spinners indeed.

Another style of double flyer wheel is shown in Fig. 27. It is reminiscent of the wheel shown in Fig. 19. This is an American style of wheel. "B. Sanford" has his named stamped on this style as well as one similar to the wheel shown in Fig. 26. With the driving wheel set above the bobbin and flyer units, one is also reminded of the Irish Castle wheel. Here, one is really aware of the combination of features from various styles of wheels which American makers tried in their search for the perfect spinning wheel.

The spinning wheel shown in Fig. 28 is a good example of what a prolific experimenter and patenter of wheels can devise. Amos Webster patented a "Linen Wheel" in 1812, but the records of these early patent wheels were lost in the disastrous Patent Office fires of the mid-nineteenth century. Three wheels with his name stamped on them are known to us. The wheel in Fig. 28, though not stamped, is identical to one of these three signed wheels except that it has two bobbin and flyer units instead of one. The driving wheel is thin, but it is made of cast iron. The small wheel above the iron wheel increases the number of flyer revolutions per driving wheel revolution dramatically. This additional wheel is usually referred to as an accelerating wheel and may have been adapted from Amos Minor's patented wool wheel head. In the next chapter we will be examining spinning wheels which used accelerating wheels and the double treadle, also noticeable on the Webster wheels.

Chapter Five

Double Treadle, Double Wheel, Flax Wheels

The group of spinning wheels shown in this chapter all have accelerating wheels and double treadles. These are two very significant contributions to the development of the spinning wheel as a tool for handspinning. The fact that textile machinery ultimately moved in very different directions from the flax wheels shown in this chapter should in no way prejudice us against the ingenuity of these wheels. The accelerating wheel allowed the wheel maker to produce a spinning wheel which required little treadling to use and yet was not so cumbersome as the large Canadian spinning wheel. The double treadle arrangement (Fig. 34) solved one of the spinner's worst complaints about the Saxony wheel. If the spinner is not careful, the driving wheel has a tendency to reverse itself causing a large mess in the hooks on the flyer. The problem is that the spinner must depress the treadle only when the axle crank is on its way down and not when it is on the way up. The double treadle solves this problem by allowing the spinner to alternate feet in the treadling process. It also allows the spinner to start the wheel going with the feet from any crank position. On the single treadle wheels the spinner must move the driving wheel by hand until the crank is in the proper position to commence spinning. This combination of features makes for a smoother, more even treadling operation, which makes it much easier to spin a nice thread.

The first wheel shown is affectionately known as the "Village Idiot's wheel" (Fig. 29). Mike, upon seeing this wheel for the first time, foolishly labelled it and predicted that no one would make two such atrocities. Two weeks later, the spinning wheel shown in Fig. 30 turned up. There are a few differences, but the same combination of wheels and mediocre craftsmanship told the tale. The "village idiot" had made two wheels. Unfortunately, he was as modest as untalented, and he didn't sign either of his works. From a distance these wheels look quite nice. An examination of Fig. 29, however, shows that he was unable to turn two front legs the same, and he was unable

43

FIGURE 29

This double treadle flax wheel with an accelerating wheel was found in New Hampshire. Our rather humorous description of this wheel and its companion piece in Figure 30 should not be missed. This one is missing the distaff assembly, but it undoubtably looked like the one in Figure 30. There is a tension device for raising the accelerating wheel as well as for the bobbin and flyer. Flax wheels with an accelerating wheel worked much better when some method for regulating the tension on the driving band between the two wheels was available. Such a tension device is found on about half of such wheels.   (Pennington Collection)

FIGURE 30

This wheel is an improvement on its companion wheel shown in Figure 29. The tension device for the bobbin and flyer works much better. It is the threaded horizontal bar in the front. The top piece of the distaff is missing, but the rest of the distaff assembly protrudes from the front wheel support about 2/3's of the way up.

(Pennington Collection)

to properly center the treadles. He did a much nicer job of making the wheel pictured in Fig. 30, and the tension device is much better. It is possible, of course, that these two wheels were made by different craftsmen, and that they represent a distinctive style of wheel. They were both found in the same general vicinity, and for the moment we believe they were the product of the same man. It certainly makes a better story.

The "village idiot" made a better spinning wheel than the fellow who made the wheel shown in Fig. 31. It is one of two such wheels reported in southern Ohio. We have not seen its mate, but do trust the person who said he had seen both of them in the same town. We hesitate to say this is an Ohio style since the vast majority of double wheels have been seen in the Northeast. The driving wheels are so light and spindly on this wheel that they have little "carry" or momentum. Unlike the "village idiot," this maker failed to include a way to adjust the tension on the driving cord or band between the two wheels. This adjustment feature, which is very important, is missing from about half of the double wheels of which we know, but it does not seem to be indicative of an older wheel by itself. The crank on the wheel shown in Fig. 31 is in front of the driving wheel and gives the reader some idea of how the double treadle relates to the crank. While this wheel is a very advanced design, it is a very poor spinner.

The splendid wheel shown in Fig. 32 is perhaps the finest spinning wheel we have ever seen in terms of both craftsmanship and design. It came out of Pennsylvania. It has the number 383 as well as some small flowers stamped in the table. It has its crank between the wheel supports, which required the maker to cut a slot in the table for the footman to pass through. It has the most positive tension device for adjusting the tension between the wheels we have seen. The tension device for the bobbin and flyer unit is similar to that employed on Saxony wheels. Dovetailing and other techniques used by quality furniture makers with a sense of permanence and pride abound in this wheel.

The two wheels from Guilford, Connecticut are fine representatives of the best known style of double wheel, the Connecticut chair wheel. This style of wheel has been found all over the Northeast and Midwest, but most of these have been traced back to the Connecticut area. These two wheels shown in Figs. 33-35 may have been made by the same man since they came out of the same town and have very similar turnings and tension devices. Unlike most chair wheels, these have: square legs, tension devices for the belt between the two wheels, and a very good tension device for the bobbin and flyer unit. Most chair wheels have a threaded nut which fastens against the front leg and keeps the mother-of-all and maidens from turning. Fig. 35 has the initials "E.L." stamped on the top of the back legs. The only other marked chair wheel we have seen had "J. Miles" stamped in it.

46

FIGURE 31

This very spindly double treadle flax wheel with an accelerating wheel has an internal crank. There is no tension device between the two wheels. The distaff was attached to the top of the front wheel support. This wheel was found in southern Ohio, and another of the same sort was reported in that area. (Pennington Collection)

47

FIGURE 32

This truly magnificent flax wheel has excellent tension devices. The distaff assembly is missing but would have been of the traditional sort. A hole for it is found near the bobbin and flyer tension device to the left of the maidens. The front maiden is cocked to the left to allow for better alignment of the bobbin and flyer. This arrangement is often found on well made wheels. This wheel has the number 383 stamped in its base. We hope that more of these wheels have survived as they would be a joy to any spinner or collector. This one was found in Pennsylvania. (Pennington Collection)

FIGURE 33

This Connecticut chair wheel is unusual in that it has solid wheels. The "chair wheel" is the most common style of double treadle accelerated flax wheel. This one and its companion piece in Figure 35 both came from the same town in Conn. The square legs are unusual as is the tension device. This style of wheel is an excellent spinner. The distaff top is not original. There is a tension device for the wheels as well as the bobbin and flyer, but many chair wheels do not have this feature. The distaff assembly may be found behind the wheels in the top horizontal bar or on the right hand horizontal arm as well as where this one is shown.   (Pennington Collection)

FIGURE 34

This view shows the back of the wheel in Figure 33 and shows the double treadle arrangement. Note the auger marks on the top wheel which suggest strongly that it was made in the 19th century.

FIGURE 35

The main difference between this chair wheel and the one in Fig. 33 is that this has the more typical wheels with spokes. Solid wheels are very unusual in any spinning wheel. This wheel like its companion wheel has two pulleys on the bobbin as well as the flyer, another unusual feature. This wheel has the initials "E.L." stamped in the top of the back two legs. Only one chair wheel we know of has a full name marked on it, "J. Miles". "E.L." are the only initials we know of. It is a mystery why the craftsmen of such fine wheels would chose to remain anonymous.   (Pennington Collection)

This style appears to be uniquely American. The origin of this style is lost, perhaps in the Patent Office fires, but it is not hard to imagine a chair-maker's influence in either the idea or the production of the early models. Because of the uniqueness of its style and its superb spinning characteristics, speculation about the age and origin of the chair wheel is a favorite sport of spinning wheel collectors. One thing we feel safe to say is that there is a close connection between Amos Minor's accelerating head for wool wheels and the accelerating wheel in flax wheels. The Webster wheels have a very small accelerating wheel (Fig. 28), which is very reminiscent of the Minor's head accelerating wheel (Fig. 37). Which came first is the big question as it affects the dating of all accelerated spinning wheels. We do know that Minor patented his wool wheel head in 1810 and possibly earlier. At any rate all double wheel flax wheels are very unusual. The chair wheel style is the only one which seems to have been popular with more than one or two makers.

Chapter Six
Wool Wheels

The wool wheel is the oldest style of spinning wheel. The most primitive spinning device is the simple drop or cup spindle. (Fig. 36) A wool wheel is made by turning such a spindle to a horizontal position and then driving it by means of a wheel and driving cord. Indian spinning wheels have no legs, but most Occidental wheels do. Perhaps, for this reason India is commonly thought of as the birthplace of the spinning wheel. A tension device is a nice addition once legs have brought the table up off the ground. After that addition, the modern wool wheel is much like its Indian predecessor with a few other frills we will discuss.

There are three main types of wool wheel head: direct drive, bat's or palm head, and Minor's head. In Fig. 34 we show them side by side for comparison. They are remarkably similar except for the accelerating wheel on the Minor's head. Technically, both the direct drive and bat's head spindles are directly driven by the driving wheel cord, but we continue to use the common terminology and hope to avoid further confusion. The built-in direct drive is the oldest form of spindle holder. The bat's head and Minor's head are inserted into a hole in the spindle post and are removable. As Fig. 37 shows, there was also a removable direct drive. The historical sequence of these three forms of head is very much open to question. Amos Minor patented his accelerated wool wheel head in 1810 or earlier. We assume his invention was practical, which would imply that there were wool wheels with holes in the spindle post already available. We have no explanation, however, as to why people would have built wool wheels with removable direct drive heads or bat's heads. We know that Minor also patented a spinning wheel of some sort in 1803, which could have been a wool wheel with a built-in Minor's head. The sequence of events is further confused by the fact that many Minor's heads have labels which claim that the accelerating head was patented in 1802. One thing is not confusing or debatable, and that is the popularity of

FIGURE 36

The drop spindle being used by Beth is not old, as they are quite rare, but the principle is apparent. This is the forerunner of the spinning wheel. Similarity between the drop spindle and the metal spindles in Figure 37 should be noted.

(Pennington Collection)

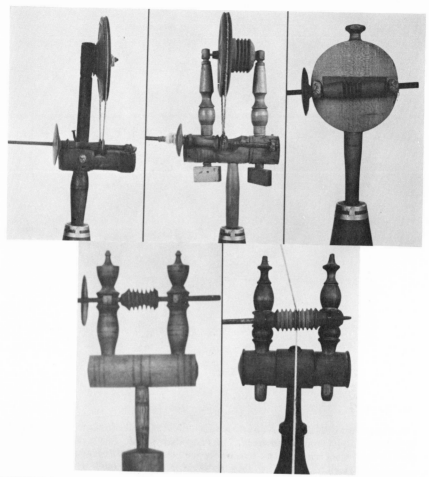

FIGURE 37

The wool wheel heads pictured represent the three main types of spindle arrangement. See the text for a fuller description of them. They are, top row, left to right: Minor's head variant, Minor's head, bat's or palm head (Shaker example); bottom row, left, removable direct drive and, right, built-in direct drive.

(Pennington Collection)

the Minor's head. Thousands were being made in factories fifty years later, and some people sought to improve on this head as the fifth head in Fig. 37 indicates.

Tension devices are almost as individual as the fingerprints of the makers. We will discuss some of the more common types as we examine particular wool wheels. Basically, there are two main types as shown in Figs. 38-39. The sliding table with a tightening nut type shown in Fig. 38 is more typical of the

55

FIGURE 38

This wool wheel with a built-in direct drive is typical of wool wheels found throughout the Midwest and Appalachian areas. The steep slant to the table is more pronounced than in most wool wheels. The tension device consists of a threaded screw with a wooden nut which fastens the sliding top table to the main table of the wheel. The sliding top table is fastened to the spindle post. This tension device is very common on these wheels as are the bulbous turnings on the spokes. The wheel rim is narrow and has a groove to keep the driving band from slipping off.   (Pennington Collection)

South and Midwest. The threaded rod through the spindle post shown in Fig. 39 is found primarily in the East.

The wool wheel pictured in Fig. 38 is of the direct drive variety. The large turnings on the spokes are not purely ornamental as they supply additional weight to the edge of the wheel, which increases the momentum of the wheel appreciably and makes the spinner's task easier. The steep slant to the table, which we refer to as rake from our hot rod adolescent days, serves no function and may or may not be evidence of an early wheel. It is true that many of the wool wheels we would call early, for other reasons, also have a lot

FIGURE 39

This wool wheel is typical of New England wheels. It has a wide rim with no groove in it. The tension device is a threaded screw above the table which pushes the spindle post away from the wheel and increases the tension on the driving band. The turnings are very restrained and the wheel support post is much less massive than its Midwestern counterparts. The bat's head is not original but is wholly appropriate as would be a Minor's head.

(Pennington Collection)

of rake. The wheel rim is only 1½ inches wide and has a groove in it to keep the driving cord on.

The wool wheel shown in Fig. 39 is very typical of wheels found in the Northeast. It has a nice bat's head and not much slant or "rake" to the table. The wheel rim is wide, nearly four inches, and consequently, there is no need for a groove in the rim. We have not been able to make any correlation between the type of wheel rim and the age of the wool wheel. Once again, the austere look of the wheel is borne out by a Massachusetts origin. This wheel has a metal wheel axle as do all but one of the wool wheels pictured in this chapter.

57

FIGURE 40

This wheel has a tension device which appears frequently in upstate New York. It has a revolving barrel with a hole in it for the spindle head. A wooden nut tightens down on the outside of a maiden to hold the rotating barrel in the proper position. It has a narrow wheel rim with a groove in it. The wheel post is intermediate in size and turnings. (Owned by Ed Penet)

The most interesting feature of the wool wheel in Fig. 40 is the tension device. It is a rotating barrel with a wooden nut tightener to hold it in the proper position. This type of tensioner was particularly popular in upstate New York.

The finely turned wheel in Fig. 41 has some additional refinements meant to be functional. The two turned horns on the sliding table were meant to hold rolags within easy reach of the spinner. The hand-carved wooden wingnut used to control the sliding table and hence the tension is set under the wheel table, thus making room for the scooped out hollow for additional rolag storage. The spindle goes directly through the maidens and does not employ the traditional braided cornhusks found on most wool wheels. The

58

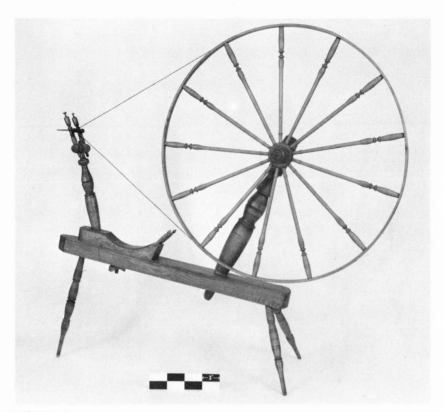

FIGURE 41

This wheel is similar to that shown in Figure 38 and came out of Pennsylvania. It has a rolag holder as well as a depression in the sliding table for piling rolags. It is very beautifully turned, and the tension nut located under the table is a beautiful carved wing nut. It has the narrow rim with a groove and a massive wheel post.

(Pennington Collection)

general look of this wheel suggests either a Midwestern or Southern origin. The wheel rim is grooved.

In Fig. 42 we see a direct drive wool wheel from Ohio. It has a grooved wheel rim and very heavy spokes. This wheel has a great deal of "carry" and spins quite nicely.

The most obvious characteristics of the wheel shown in Fig. 43 is the round, turned table. It has a very large wheel as the picture indicates. It has a flat wide rim. The tension device is a rotating barrel with a nut tightener. Unlike the wheel in Fig. 40 the spindle post is single. The purpose of the handle on the table is probably for stability in moving the wheel about the

59

FIGURE 42

From what has been said about other wool wheels you should know that this wheel is probably Midwestern with a narrow grooved wheel rim with a sliding table tension device. It came out of Ohio and has a built-in direct drive. It is a very good spinner with good momentum to the wheel due to the large turnings on the wheel spokes.

(Pennington Collection)

house. One other such round-tabled wool wheel is reported. They appear to be Midwestern in origin.

The wheel pictured in Fig. 44 appears normal at first glance. It has a wooden wheel axle and chamfered legs which probably indicates an 18th century wheel, but the hole in the spindle post casts doubt on such an assumption. The real oddity of this wheel is the reversed legs. We have heard of others with this malady but have not seen them. In one way this is a slight improvement. The clumsy spinner is less likely to stumble over a wheel leg while spinning. (Hence, Mike sold it to Dave.)

60

FIGURE 43

The round table makes this wool wheel very unusual. It has a very large wheel and is very simple in design. It was found in Michigan. It has a rotating barrel attached to a single post for a tension device. There has been one other sighted in the Michigan area, and none elsewhere are known.   (Pennington Collection)

The wool wheel has a basic style, which should be apparent from an examination of the pictures. It is a three-legged animal on this side of the Atlantic. The only variation in the table is the rake and the shape. This wheel does what it is designed to do quite well. We have seen evidence that it was being made right into this century. There was some disenchantment with the constant standing in the use of this style of wheel as Chapters 8 and 9 will show, but mechanized multiple spinning units put this style in its grave and not a superior style of single spindle spinner.

FIGURE 44

This wool wheel has some very primitive features on it which lead us to believe it is one of the older wheels we have seen. It has a wooden axle for the wheel instead of the more usual metal axle. The legs are chamfered instead of turned. The most notable feature, however, is the reversal of the usual leg pattern. It has two high legs under the spindle with a single leg under the wheel. Other examples of this variation are known. This one came from Maine, and the others were reported in Mass.

(Pennington Collection)

Chapter Seven
Shaker Spinning Wheels

The Shakers are a communal religious group famous for their fine furniture. During their heyday in the late 18th and 19th centuries, they were among the finest furniture makers in the world. Much attention has been paid to their chair-making industry, but they should be better recognized for their contribution to the textile industry as spinning wheel makers. Soon after they were gathered into communities by Father Joseph Meacham in the 1780's, they started making wheels, not only for their own use, but also for sale to the rest of the world. Elder David Meacham, the first Shaker trustee at New Lebanon, had his initials placed on many wool wheels made at that community over the next fifty years. It now appears likely that his initials were a kind of quality control mark which assured the buyer that the wheel was one of high quality. Trustees at other communities, such as Deacon Francis Winkley of Canterbury, New Hampshire, followed Meacham's example. Some wheels identical to those stamped with trustee initials have been found without initials, and it is theorized that these wheels were made for use by the community.

Many more examples of Shaker wool wheels exist than flax wheels. We have concentrated our text and pictures on wool wheels for this reason. They are among the simplest and most beautiful wheels ever made, and fortunately they are among the most common. Many of these are unmarked, but a close comparison with marked wheels usually provides easy identification. The first wheel shown is a Francis Winkley wheel and is marked with a small "F.W." stamped in the end grain of the table near the tension device. This wheel had a horn collar around the top of the spindle post. Fig. 45 shows this wheel, but the collar is missing. Some wheels of his have a pewter collar as do the wheels of other Shaker makers. The existence of a bone collar is not a sure sign of a Shaker wool wheel, but it is a good clue.

FIGURE 45

This wool wheel was made by the Shakers in Canterbury, N.H. and is stamped "F.W." Francis Winkley was a trustee in that community before 1847 and his initials appear on many wool and flax wheels produced there. (Pennington Collection)

Different communities used different types of tension devices, and the same community may have used different types. The David Meacham wool wheel (not shown) seems to have an odd type of tension device which is seen only on New Lebanon wool wheels. The Canterbury wheels all appear to use the common style of Eastern tension device. Sabbathday Lake, Maine wool wheels are not often marked and have several different types of tension device. They do have horn or pewter collars in most cases. The wool wheel shown in Fig. 47 has the initial "SR AL", which is very common on flax wheels as well. The initials belong to Deacon Samuel Ring, a trustee of the Alfred, Maine community. Many flax wheels of the type shown in Fig. 48 with his initials exist. The distinguishing characteristic of these flax wheels is a pronounced thickening of the treadle piece connecting with the footman.

64

FIGURE 46   (Photo by David Serette)

An unusual under the table tension device wool wheel from the Sabbathday Lake Shaker Community.

This permits the left foot of the spinner to rest securely on the treadle pieces while the right foot rests on the treadle proper. The first wheel with this arrangement appears to be an unmarked wheel in the Sabbathday Lake collection which is attributed to Elder Oliver Holmes of the Sabbathday Lake community in 1796. It has the same turnings on the maidens as the SR AL wheels.

Other wool wheels from the Sabbathday Lake collection are shown to give the collector an idea of the variation in design among Shaker wool wheels. This variation in style is easily understandable when you consider that there was a continuous tradition of spinning wheel production among the Shakers for over 80 years and that most of the 10 New England communities were involved in this production. Some makers, such as Benjamin Bailey of the

FIGURE 47

The "SR AL" wool wheel was produced in the Alfred, Maine Shaker Community ("AL") and was stamped with the initials of Samual Ring ("SR") a member of that community from 1784-1848.   (Pennington Collection)

Alfred community, made as many as 700 wheels during their productive lives. It is no wonder that Mike while in the East for four years doing research became convinced that as many as one in four of the wool wheels he saw were Shaker made.

The Shakers also had communities in the Midwest, but as yet we are not in a position to comment authoritatively on the production of these communities. We know that an extensive silk industry was carried on by the two Shaker communities in Kentucky as well as by several in Ohio. The museum at Pleasant Hill, housing many Kentucky Shaker artifacts, has several wheels similar in principle to the wheel shown in Fig. 58 although these are mounted

FIGURE 48

This is a Shaker flax wheel bearing the same initials "SR AL" (see Figure 47). It is an excellent wheel in all respects. The earliest known wheel of this style was made by Oliver Holmes of the Sabbathday Lake Community and dates from 1796. It is still in the Sabbathday Lake Collection.

(Taylor Collection)

FIGURE 49

"B.B." are the initials on this Shaker wool wheel and they belonged to Benjamin Baily who was also at Alfred between 1799-1880. (Pennington Collection)

on long boards in a slightly different manner than the threaded rod shown in our illustration. Hopefully, more information will appear about the spinning wheels of the Midwestern Shaker communities.

The Shakers are a noble people who have supported many humanitarian causes while faithfully serving God through the inspiration of the life of Mother Ann Lee. We think their humility and hard work are truly expressed in the careful labor they expended in creating not only very beautiful, but also very functional spinning wheels. The "SR AL" flax wheel is the finest Saxony flax wheel we have ever used. Shaker wool wheels are generally in excellent condition when found. The wheels are not warped or split, and the tension devices work well. Mother Ann Lee can certainly be proud of her "children's" work.

FIGURE 50

(Photo by David Serette)

This Shaker wool wheel is marked "J.H." (John Holmes) and is one of many of this design in the Sabbathday Lake Collection. John Holmes (1783-1854), one of a most gifted family which included the wheel maker Oliver Holmes, was Deacon of the Church Family at Sabbathday Lake from 1821 to 1830.

(Photo by David Serette)

FIGURE 51

Shaker Flax Wheel from Sabbathday Lake Collection. Distaff not all original.

FIGURE 52   (Photo by David Serette)

Shaker Flax Wheel from Sabbathday Lake Collection.

FIGURE 53

The L. Wight pendulum wheel is a "sitting" wool wheel. The spinner sits with the wheel on his right and turns the wheel by hand. The treadle, when depressed by the foot causes the spindle to move away from the spinner. This action duplicates that achieved by walking away from the spindle in the typical wool wheels. The Wight wheel also comes with a smaller size wheel depending on which of the two factories made it. These wheels are among the earliest patent wheels we have much information about and they still exist in numbers sufficient enough to lead us to believe that they enjoyed some real popularity. The patent we have examined was taken out in 1856.

(Pennington Collection)

Chapter Eight
Patent Wheels

The Minor's head opened the way for a whole wave of attempted improvements on the wool wheel. Some of these were patented, and some were not. In this chapter we will look at some of these attempts. The wool wheel had basically the same style for hundreds of years, but in the latter half of the 19th century American makers made radical changes in the basic style we have observed in the last chapter. All of the spinning wheels shown in this chapter have the familiar spindle observed in the last 2 chapters. The wool wheel is a large machine, so it is natural that some of the attempts to improve the wool wheel would include a reduction in size. The other drawback to the wool wheel is that the spinner must remain standing while spinning, hence its nickname the walking wheel.

The L. Wight wool wheel, also known as the "pendulum wheel", in Fig. 53 appears to have been the most popular of the odd wool wheels. It was patented in 1856. We know of at least 10 specimens of this wheel which have survived. They were made in both New York and Wisconsin. The name "J. Waite" appears on the Wisconsin wheels, but we think he was a distributor or patent purchaser. The only difference in the wheels produced in these two locations is the size of the driving wheel. The only advantage in this style is that it eliminates the need for the spinner to stand or walk. The spindle is located at the end of a long arm. By depressing a treadle with the foot the spinner is able to move the spindle away at a controlled rate. Then having spun the wool, the spinner can release the treadle slowly and wind the spun wool on the spindle without leaving the seat. The spinner still turns the driving wheel by hand. The weight's function is to return the spindle when the treadle is released.

The wheel in Fig. 54 was endowed by its inventor, S. Dell, with many of the same features as the Wight wheel. The basic difference is that Dell's spindle arm was hinged at the bottom rather than at the top. They both possess the

FIGURE 54

The S. Dell "lever action spinner" has a plate on it which indicates it was patented, but no number is given and the patent office has not been able to track down any information about it. Perhaps the records were lost in the patent office fires of the mid-19th century which consumed so much spinning wheel lore. It is an ungainly monster taking up much space, and it is not surprising that we have seen only this one example. The principle behind it is similar to the L. Wight wheel, and perhaps it is an unsuccessful copy of that pendulum wheel. Note that like the Wight wheel, the Dell wheel has an accelerating head a long way from the spindle.   (Pennington Collection)

accelerating principle of Amos Minor. Apparently, Dell did not patent this wheel as no evidence of such a patent has yet surfaced.

The J. Bryce wheel shown in Fig. 55 is a late patent wheel (1872). It is designed to clamp on a table. The driving wheel is metal as is most of the wheel. It has no driving cord but relies on a friction system to provide power to the spindle. It is a very practical portable wheel, which had it appeared earlier might have been a very popular item. It definitely solved the size difficulty; however, the spinner had to remain within an arm's length of the

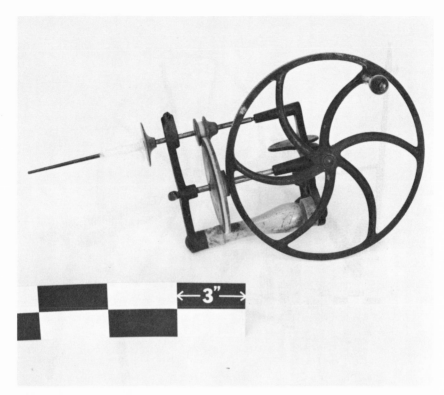

FIGURE 55

The J. Bryce patent wheel of 1872 was made in Grand Haven, Michigan. We have seen a few, but its late date appears to have doomed it. Note the extremely small size and the table clamp. It is the only wheel we have seen which does not use a driving cord or band but relies solely on friction between its wheels. It works quite well as a quiller, but it is difficult to use as a wool wheel since one is soon too far away from the wheel to use it in the normal course of spinning wool.   (Pennington Collection)

machine. Such a proximity requirement forced the spinner to alternate between spinning and winding on the spun wool quite often. The scarcity of this wheel is probably attributable to both this drawback and the end of handspinning at the end of the 19th century.

The Hathorn spinner in Fig. 56-57 is also a clamp-on table model. It is possible that Hathorn was an alias of Rube Goldberg if this wheel is any evidence. The wheel employs a standard model Minor's head. After that, it gets a little complicated. In Fig. 56 it is shown in position to spin. The "windmill" is a winder, and the small metal arm, sticking out beyond the spindle, aids in the winding process. There is a metal counting-mechanism attached to the winder post. In Fig. 57 it is set up as a combination swift and quill winder. Hathorn's wheel is undoubtably versatile. It was patented in

FIGURES 56 and 57

Hathorn's American Spinner is one late patent wheel that had some little success. The one shown has the production number 4109 stamped on it in three places; the wheel hub, the table, and the winder post. Most of those we have seen have a paper label giving instructions for the use of the various apparati included in this marvelous machine. As shown in Figure 56, it is a combination wool wheel and winder. Note the small guide for the wool to go from spindle to winder. It is a wire loop extending out to the left of the spindle of the Minor's head. In Figure 57, the wheel has become a combination quiller and swift. There are many holes in the table. The post with the

76

winder on it has dowels on the botton and on the back which permit it to lie or stand securely. The tension device consists of several holes in the table into which the Minor's head is stuck until one which gives good tension is found. It is a remarkably crude tension device for a wheel which attempted to do so much. These wheels were made in Bangor, Maine in the 1870's. The original patent is available from the patent office and makes humorous and cryptic reading. There is a cloverleaf shaped hole in the center of the table which was undoubtedly for a table clamp, but we cannot envision a clamp in that position that would work well.

(Taylor/Pennington Collection)

FIGURE 57

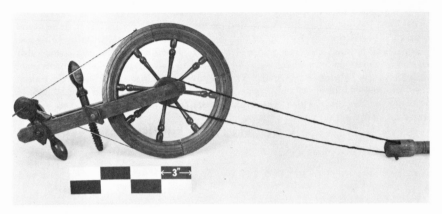

FIGURE 58

Strictly speaking this wheel is not a patent wheel. It is an odd portable wool wheel like the last two wheels shown. It was secured to some sort of base by means of the wooden threaded rod. The wheel shown is an accelerating head. The spinner attaches the pulley shown at the right, and the wheel. Then he pulls on the clothesline-line cord stretched between the pulley and the wheel. The large accelerating wheel is necessary because of the inefficiency of the motion in pulling the clothesline. Wheels similar in principle to this one, but mounted on long boards were used by the Shakers in Kentucky for spinning silk. (Pennington Collection)

1871 and combines more functions in a small space than any other wheel we have seen or can imagine. It also came too late to make a lasting impression on the spinning wheel market.

The wheel shown in Fig. 58 is a large accelerating head. It was meant to be clamped to a table. There was no large driving wheel; instead, the power was supplied to the accelerating head wheel by a continuous cord which stretched from wheel hub to an independent pulley attached several feet away. It is little wonder few examples of this style have survived. There are several variations of this hand-pulled continuous cord style of wheel. Some of them were used for wool as the one shown was, and some may have been used by the Shakers in Kentucky in their silk spinning. This style does not appear to be regionally specific. It is probably a later effort but is not patented, so we have no definite date for any models of this style.

We have shown a very small sample of the total number of wheels patented. Many of those patented may never have gone into production. Others were produced in such small numbers that no examples survive. The ones we have shown give a good indication of American ingenuity. It is unfortunate but true that some patent wheels we have seen are obvious copies of other, earlier patent wheels. S. Dell may be one example of such idea thievery. Even the grand world of spinning wheels has been occasionally profaned by its two-legged creator.

Chapter Nine
Canadian Wheels

The final stages in the use of spinning wheels for the spinning of wool occurred late in the 19th century. The patent wool wheels and other oddities we looked at in the last chapter were the last gasp of the single unit spindle mechanism. The 18th century had witnessed the birth of the multiple unit spindle mechanism. Hargraves, Arkwright, and Crompton are all important names in that story. The spinning jenny, mule, and jack were the machines which took over the spinning of wool as well as cotton. Their story is one told elsewhere, but it meant the end of hand-spinning as surely as the automobile doomed the horse.

In this chapter we look at the last stage in the development of the Saxony wheel and its bobbin and flyer unit. The wheels shown in Fig. 59-60 are Canadian in origin. They feature large driving wheels, orifices, and hooks. They are superb spinners of wool. The lack of a distaff along with the changes in the bobbin and flyer unit indicate that these were intended to be sit-down wool spinners. It should be noted that many European wheels had no distaff assembly as a part of the wheel, even though they were flax wheels. European spinners leaned toward the use of free-standing distaffs; some of which are seen in the Horner collection.

The Canadian wheels were often painted with buttermilk paints as well as other paints of several colors. Green, yellow, and orange predominated. The tension devices were very simple in most cases, and the two wheels shown are typical in that respect. A few Canadian wheels have a threaded tension device, but most have a rotating mother-of-all with a metal wingnut to keep the mother-of-all from slipping. The wood in them is often pine. The turnings are very crude, but the wheels work beautifully. The wheel shown in Fig. 59 is very typical of the Canadian wheels which have flooded antique shops of late. It is orange, "rough", and a fine spinner.

The wheel shown in Fig. 60 has a much larger driving wheel than most.

FIGURE 59

This typical Canadian wheel is painted a light orange. Unlike wheels from the United States, Canadian wheels were often painted. They were used for wool spinning and were made in the late 19th and early 20th century. They have very large wheels, big hooks, and large orifices. The tension device is a wire clamp or metal wing nut arrangement as in this wheel. The wing nut is loosened and the mother-of-all is pushed back away from the wheel. These wheels are excellent wool spinners, and people who wish to produce a lot of wool are well advised to find one of these. They are extremely plentiful and have little antique value.   (Pennington Collection)

FIGURE 60

This unpainted pine wheel from Canada is unusual in that it is a double treadle Saxony wheel. It has the wire clamp tension device. The wheel is even larger than most Canadian style wheels. This wheel is the fastest spinner we have ever had the thrill of keeping up with.   (Owned by Kathy Edleman Hutchinson)

FIGURE 61

This large flax brake is used to break up the outer husk and inner cortex of the flax plant. There are several parallel boards which fit between one another and force the flax into a series of right angles. The large hammer at the end helps break up the husk. (Pennington Collection)

These larger driving wheels seem to be associated with metal treadles and in general more recent wheels. The double treadle arrangement on this wheel is not unique but is uncommon. This wheel is undoubtedly the fastest spinner we have ever encountered, including the accelerated wheels. The large driving wheel and double treadle account for this speed. The tension device is similar to the one in Fig. 59 but features more metal in it. This is in keeping with the increasing use of metal parts, which is typical of late Canadian wheels.

Chapter Ten

Miscellaneous Equipment

This chapter has a twofold function. First, it should help to acquaint people with some of the equipment used by spinners in preparing the flax or wool for spinning or for transferring the spun material to looms for weaving. Second, we hope to correctly identify some items which have been confused with spinning wheels. We begin with those items used in conjunction with flax spinning and then move to those used with wool spinning or both.

The flax brake in Fig. 61 is a nice example of the machine used to "break" or loosen the outer husk and inner core from the useful fiber. The hammer on the end is used first, and then the bundle of flax is laid across the parallel slats and the top slats lowered onto the bundle. The brake was used after a ripple was used to remove the seeds. The top item in Fig. 62 is the type of thing which might have been used to "ripple" the flax. The scrutching knife was used to beat the "broken" flax to remove the loose husks and cores from it. Several examples of this wooden implement are shown in Fig. 62. The hackels or hetchels in Fig. 62 are used to remove the loose husks or short broken fibers from the bundle of flax after it has been scrutched. The hackler, hetchler, heckler (yes, that is the origin of the word) usually had a set of hackles ranging from metal spikes set close together to far apart.

The wool cards seen in Fig. 63 are quite commonly seen in antique stores. Some of them are labelled "cotton cards", and the maker usually knows. Cotton cards have smaller hooks. These cards are used to prepare the wool for spinning. Through the use of the cards the carder realigns the wool fibers so that they are parallel to one another. This simplifies the spinner's task considerably. Fig. 64 shows wool combs used to prepare worsted wool. This was an additional step which produced a smoother and finer yarn when spun.

The winder shown in Fig. 65 could be used for either flax or wool. It is a counting device for the spinner to determine how much length is in a skein of wool or flax. Many winders are two yards around the arms. Most winders

FIGURE 62

The comb-like object to the top left is the type of instrument used to take the seeds off the flax plant prior to using the flax brake. These instruments were called ripples. The seeds were used to replant next year. An instrument of similar design was used in the making of straw brooms, so we are tentative in calling the one shown a "ripple". The two wooden knives are scrutching knives and were used after the flax brake to knock off the pieces of husk and cortex that remained after the breaking process. The bottom two boards with spikes driven through them are hackles (spelling optional according to locale). The beautiful tiger striped example with a dove-tailed box to protect the spikes is stamped F.A. Goodrich who was a Shaker at Mount Lebanon. Several sizes of hackles were used in separating the short fibered tow from the longer fibered flax. The finer toothed hackles were used last.

(Pennington Collection)

also have a clicker inside of them to indicate when the winder has been turned forty times. Generalizations about winders are hard to make because of the great variety of styles and because different counting systems were used in different areas of the country at different times. We have given the characteristics of the most common type found in this country. The niddy noddies in Fig. 63 are also yarn winders of a crude sort. Most of these are also two yards around. It is unlikely that anyone has been confused by a yarn winder, but odder things have happened to us on collecting expeditions. So

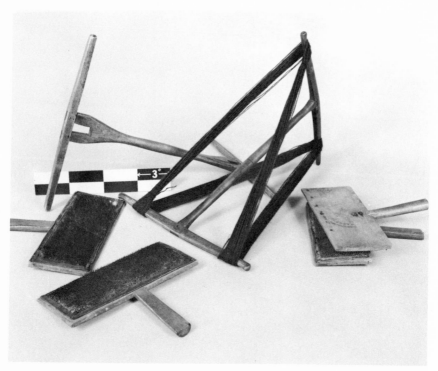

FIGURE 63

The top two T-shaped objects are primitive yarn winders called niddy noddies. The one with yarn around it shows how they were wrapped. One complete revolution was approximately 2 yards although smaller 1½ yards models are known. The paddles with wire teeth set in leather are wool or cotton cards and are used to make the fibers parallel to one another for easier spinning. The cotton cards have smaller teeth than the wool cards. Both form the material into rolags which are rolls of fibers about 8" in length.

(Pennington Collection)

for the record, those things which look like little windmills are not spinning wheels.

The squirrel cage swift in Fig. 66 should be called an unwinder. Its function is to take highly unmanageable skeins of flax or wool and make it possible for the weaver to load her bobbins or quills. Knitters like these for making balls of yarns out of skeins. The one shown is nearly six feet tall, which is abnormally large. Either one or both of the revolving barrels is adjustable up or down to allow the skein to be put on properly. This machine has been confused with a spinning wheel, but, of course, you wouldn't make that mistake now, would you?

Umbrella swifts (Fig. 67) don't look anything like squirrel cage swifts, but as their name implies, they do the same thing. The skein was looped over the

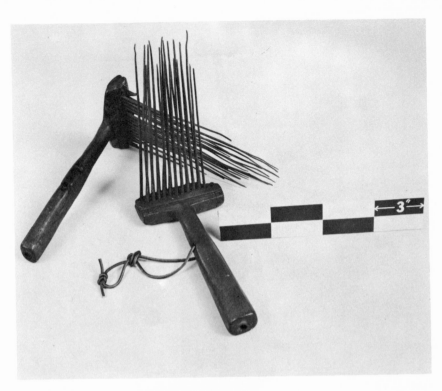

FIGURE 64

These wicked looking instruments are wool combs and were used in preparing the longer fibered worsted wools. They were heated prior to use. One of the two was mounted on a post, and the comber used the other to comb out the long fibers into parallel rolags for spinning. (Pennington Collection)

swift which was then raised like an umbrella. The swift was usually clamped to a table, and then the yarn unwound. Some of these pieces were made of scrimshaw and are avidly sought by collectors.

The quill winder shown in Fig. 68 is easy to mistake for a small wool wheel. In fact, it is possible that some were used as children's wool wheels, but that would be a rare occurrence. They were used by weavers to wind wool or flax onto quills or bobbins. In profile they do look like wool wheels, but the large thick spindle is a giveaway where it is still with the winder. The smaller wheel often has a wooden handle or a hole in a wheel spoke where a handle once was, and this is a characteristic of a quill winder that remains after the spindle assembly has been lost. Most of them have very wide-set maidens. The one shown is marked, "H. Thomson" and we have an example of his wool wheel as well. It is not surprising that one person would be making both items since

86

FIGURE 65

This six armed winder is approximately two yards around. A clicking mechanism indicates when 40 revolutions have been made. The white circle on the front is a dial for a small "clock" which indicates how many revolutions have been made since the last "click". The purpose of the yarn winder is to let the user know how much yarn he has.　　　　　　　　　　　　　　　　　　　　　　　　(Pennington Collection)

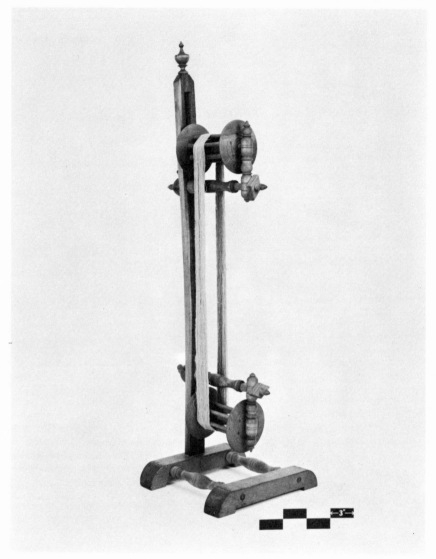

FIGURE 66

This instrument is a squirrel cage swift. It is an "unwinder". The counted skein of wool is placed over the cages as shown. The cages can be brought close together to accommodate various sizes of skein. This particular model is nearly six feet high which is very unusual. It came from Pennsylvania. It is not a vertical spinning wheel.

(Pennington Collection)

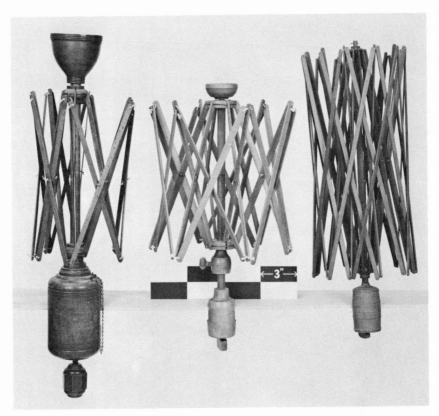

FIGURE 67

These are umbrella swifts. The skein of wool is placed over the swift and then it is opened until it holds the skein firmly. These swifts are often clamped to the table or occasionally have bases as the one on the left in the picture. The Shakers at Hancock made a great many of these, and they were usually stained yellow. The center swift is Shaker. (Pennington Collection)

89

FIGURE 68

This Quill winder could have been used as a child's wool wheel but was intended to wind quills to fit in weaving shuttles or bobbins to fit on a scarne. Marked "H. Thomson." (Pennington Collection)

FIGURE 69

This flyer and bobbin from a tow wheel would have been attached directly to the side of a small flax type wheel. This would form a very large flyer and bobbin combination with the wheel acting as the pulley. The whole mechanism was then set in a framework and treadled to spin the tow. (Pennington Collection)

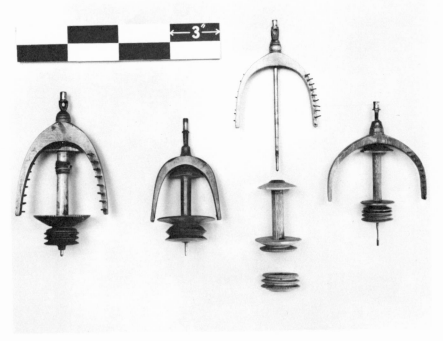

FIGURE 70

These flyer and bobbin combinations are shown for comparison. From left to right they are: Canadian, European, American showing flyer, bobbin, and flyer whorl, and a very wide American. (Pennington Collection)

they are very similar structurally. See also Fig. 71 for an accelerated Shaker quill winder.

Other items which might be confused with spinning wheels occasionally appear, but a quick check for a spinning mechanism or the area where it would be will tell the inquirer if the machine is a spinning wheel. Tow wheels, which have very large bobbin and flyers, are very rare. They were used to spin low quality flax called tow, into a crude coarse fiber used for sacks and shoelaces among other things. A bobbin and flyer from such a tow spinner is shown in Fig. 69. Tow wheels take several different forms but the size of the flyer is the tipoff.

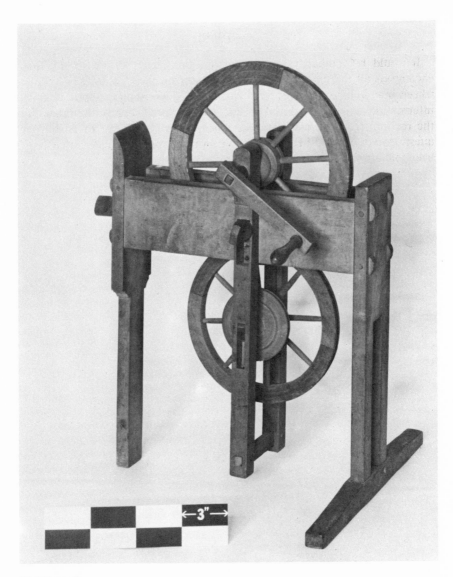

FIGURE 71

An Accelerated Shaker quill or bobbin winder of unusual design. Nicely made. Missing the spindle assembly. (Photo by David Serette - Sabbathday Lake Collection)

93

Epilog

It would be foolhardy to assume that the wheels shown in this book encompass all the types made, especially during the "Patent Era". Patent wheels may well be the basis for a second book. We shall continue to collect information on wheels and makers and would appreciate any assistance from the reader. We welcome correspondence and will attempt to answer any questions not covered here. The whole story of spinning in America hasn't been told but we hope that this will serve as a first step.

Bibliography

ABBOTT, Charles Greeley, D.Sc., ed. *Smithsonian Scientific Series.* Vol. 12, (pp. 265-300). Smithsonian Institution Series, Inc., 1932.

BROWN, Harriette J. *Hand Weaving for Pleasure and Profit.* New York and Evanston, 1952.

BUEL, Elizabeth C.B. *Tale of the Spinning Wheel.* Litchfield, Conn., 1903.

CHANNING, Marion L. *The Magic of Spinning.* Marion, Mass., 1966.

CHANNING, Marion L. *Textile Tools of Colonial Homes.* Marion, Mass., 1969.

CROWFOOT, Grace M. *Methods of Hand Spinning in Egypt and the Sudan.* Halifax, 1931.

DALBEY, Alice. "Spinning by the Turn of a Wheel or the Drop of a Spindle," Americana, Vol. 2, No. 3 (July, 1974), 16-19.

DANILOFF, Serge. "Some Rare Spinning Wheels," Antiques, Vol. 16, 1929.

DAVENPORT, Elsie. *Your Handspinning.* London, 1953.

EARL, Alice Morse. *Home Life in Colonial Days.* New York, 1898.

EATON, Allen H. *Handicrafts of the Southern Highlands.* Russell Sage Foundation, 1937.

FENNELLY, Catherine, ed. *Textiles in New England.* Old Sturgridge, Inc., 1961.

GRASSETT, K. *Complete Guide to Hand Spinning.* London, 1971.

HORNER, John. *The Linen Trade of Europe During the Spinning Wheel Period.* Belfast, 1920.

Bibliography (Cont.)

McGOWAN, Ellen Beers and WAITE, Charlotte A. *Textiles and Clothing.* New York, 1921.

MERRIMACK VALLEY TEXTILE MUSEUM. *Wool Technology and the Industrial Revolution.* Merrimack Valley Textile Museum, 1965.

PENDLETON WOOLEN MILLS. *The Wool Story...from Fleece to Fashion.* Pendleton Woolen Mills, 1965.

RALPH, William. "The Spinning Wheel — A Neglected Tool," The Chronicle of the Early American Industries Association, Inc., Vol. XXV, No. 2, (June, 1972), 22-27.

ROGERS, Horatio, M.D. "S.D. Stevens and His Spinning Wheel Collection," Essex Institute Historical Collections, Vol. CV, No. 1, January, 1969.

SCHILLER, Elaine Z. "Acadian Cotton Spinning," Shuttle, Spindle and Dyepot. Handweavers Guild of America, Inc., Vol. V, No. 3, Issue 19, (Summer 1974) p. 75.

SPENCER, Audrey. *Spinning and Weaving at Upper Canada Village.* Toronto, 1968.

————. "Spinning Wheels." Handweaver & Craftsman, Vol. 7, No. 2, Spring 1956.

THOMPSON, G.B., ed. *Spinning Wheels (The John Horner Collection).* Ulster Museum, Belfast, 1964.

WHITE, Lynn, Jr. *Medieval Technology and Social Change.* Oxford University Press, 1962.

WIGGINTON, Eliot, ed. *Foxfire 2.* Garden City, New York, 1973.

Appendix "A"

Markings Found on
Spinning Wheels and Accessories

A.A.
E.A. Bats head only
J.A. Wool
J.A. Flax
Samuel Adams
Thomas Aiken
William Allison
Nathaniel Averill

A.B.
B.B.
BMB
M.M.B. 1841 501
I.B. 1834
J.B.
Samuel Baker
Joel Baldwin
M. Ball Warrented
S. Barnum
Benjamin Baley
Allen Bangs
Turner Barns
T & G. Beggs
M.C. Beims
J. Bell
William Bissell
Silus Black
W. Blayney
Frans Boegteli
Samuel Bradeen
Z. Bradley
Conrad Bream
Ingwart Broderson
J. Brown
Brown's Vertical Spinner
Jedediah Browning
J. Bryce

Thomas Burkett
J.W. Burkhart
John Bushwell
David Butner
Jesse Buyrkrt

J C
T.C.
Sidney Campbell
W. Carr
Alfred Chamberlain
Allison Chamberlain
Jonas Child
Chipman
Eli Church
S.W. Clark
Ludwig Climer
James Cochran, Jr.
Peter Coffin
Charles L. Cole
Courier
James Crunk
Michael Crunk
David Currant

L.D.
N.D.
Daniel Danner
S. Dell Lever Spinning Wheel
Demming & Pierce Co.
A.F. Dietz
Henry B. Dobson
Douglass
Dow
Nathaniel Draper
William Dumont
W. Dunshee

Enoch Eastman
Versal Eastman
John Eden
Joshua Eden

J. Farnham
Abijah Feltch
Ferguson
Fields and Brown
Jacob Fiester
J.M. Flood
George Fox
Nathaniel Freeman
Henry Furr

J D G
Gardner
James Gibson
Ranson Bilman
E. Goodrich
John Graham
John Green
I. Gregg
Samuel Gregg
Greggs
A.H. 1816
J.H.
O. Hagen
Harmonu
Joel Hatch
G.H. Hathorn
Gideon Haven
Obediah Higinbotham
John Hill
S. Hillard
Thomas Holland
Oliver Holmes
S. Hood
Benjamin Pierce Hopkins
E. Hopkins
Howe Hopkins
Jonathan Hopkins
Richard Henry Hopkins
Richard Hopkins, Jr.
Samuel F. Hopkins
William Hopkins
William W. Hopkins
T. Dwight Hotchkiss

Thomas Howland
Warren Huse

James L. Johnson
Moses Johnson
James Johnston
Thomas Johnston
Isaac Jones

A.K.
G.K.
TK
Keisling and Babb
W. Kelia
Keller
J. Killian
Joseph Kimball
B. Klein
H. Koeller
Johannes Krause

D.L.
M. L.
1817 H. La. N. 576
John Laine
J. Leicht
W.H. Logan

Abiel McGroger
David McKeeken
Nathaniel McKeeken
Murdock McLeod
Richard McNemar
DM
HM
I.M.
I A M 1843
S.M.
W.M.
William Main
Chelton Matheny
Rawley Matthews
A. Meinecke & Son
Granville Merrill
George Metcalf
J. Miles
Henry Miller
Daniel Miltimore

Amos Miner
John Mitchell
I. Montgomery
F.D. Moore
Charles Moorehead
Morehouse & Co.
S. Morison
I. Morris
Frederick Mueller
John W. Mullens

William Nelson
J. Newby 1841
Timothy Newell
L. Norcross
Paul Nowell
Nuete's Combines Spins

Odell and Grover
A.P.
D.P.
EP NH
S.P.
I. Parish
Ashel Parmelee
Karsten Petersen
James Philpot
Alfred Pierce
B. Pierce
E.P. Pierce
E.P. Pierce, Jr.
F.B. Pierce
Fred B. Pierce
John Pierce
Joseph Pike
Jeremiah Pike Sr. and Jr.
Moses Pike
Ashel P. Porter
J. Pote
J. Prat
Casper Pringle
Amos Purdington

H.R.
SR AL
Harmonie G.R. 1823
Hugh Ramsey
James Ramsey

William Ramsey
Daniel Read
J Reynolds
Frederick Rhodes
James Rice
Thomas Ricker
Thomas Rickerin
James Rowe
John Rowell
J.Z. Rust

(A or C or T) CS
E.S.
I.S.
J S
P.S.
S.S.
B. Sanford
I. Sanford
J. Sanford
Rufus Sayward
P. Scharfer
B. Schreiber
D. Shaw
Jacob Shaw, Jr.
J. Shell
John Sherman
Barton Skinner
William Smith
Joseph Soll
John Stabb
E. Stone
E. Stone Warrented
G. Wood
N. Stone
S. Stone
John Sturtevant

A T
I T
W O T 1828
Thayer
L. Thomas
D. Thomas
D.H. Thomas
T. Thompson
H. Thomson
A. Todd

Trond
George Trowbridge
Mickjah Tucker

James Vernon

A.W. (on a distaff)
D.W. 1844
E.W.
F.W.
Z.W.
Walter Walker
John Warburton
Luther Warner
A. Webster

A. Wheeler
H.F. Wheeler
Lyman Wight
A & A Wilder or
   Azel Wilder
E.S. Williams
Frances Winkley (F.W.)
Wilson and Fairbanks
P. Wood
Phineas Wood
Wright & McAlister
Zadock Wright (Z.W.)

D. Yoder

Patented Wheels (Partial List)

Barnes	69387 in 1867	Matheny	96937 in 1869
Brain	59210 in 1866	McLoed	156203 in 1874
Burkhart	81594 in 1868	Miller	71897 in 1867
Byrkit	50094 in 1856	Moore	74115 in 1868
Clark	71047 in 1868	Moorehead	43327 in 1864
Cochran	129459 in 1872	Mullens	179043 in 1876
Cole	84261 in 1868	Odell and Glover	56600 in 1866
David Currant	7614 in 1850	Rice	96619 in 1869
Flood	51532 in 1865	Rowe	70622 in 1867
Huse	108356 in 1870	Shaw	5847 in 1848
Johnson	109116 in 1870	Walker	154969(?) in 1874
Johnston & Foust	83970 in 1868	Wheeler	4892 in 1846
Koeller	57336 in 1866	Wilson & Fairbanks	58015 in 1866
Main	103906 in 1870	Woboleti	69728 in 1867
Matheny	27059 in 1860	Wight	14482 in 1856
Matheny	62351 in 1867		